SNAKES

— BUILT FOR THE HUNT —

by Tammy Gagne

Consultant: Joe Maierhauser, CEO
Terry Phillip, Curator of Reptiles
Reptile Garden, Rapid City, South Dakota

CAPSTONE PRESS
a capstone imprint

First Facts are published by Capstone Press,
1710 Roe Crest Drive, North Mankato, Minnesota 56003
www.capstonepub.com

Library of Congress Cataloging-in-Publication Data
Gagne, Tammy, author.
  Snakes : built for the hunt / by Tammy Gagne.
      pages cm. — (First facts. Predator profiles)
  Summary: "Informative, engaging text and vivid photos introduce readers to the predatory
lives of snakes"—Provided by publisher.
  Audience: Ages 6-9
  Audience: K to grade 3
  ISBN 978-1-4914-5039-0 (library binding)
  ISBN 978-1-4914-5083-3 (eBook PDF)
1. Snakes—Juvenile literature. 2. Predation (Biology)—Juvenile literature. I. Title.
  QL666.O6G154 2016
  597.96—dc23   2015006662

Editorial Credits
Brenda Haugen, editor; Juliette Peters, designer;
Tracy Cummins, media researcher; Katy LaVigne, production specialist

Photo Credits
Alamy: blickwinkel, 6; Dreamstime: Maria Dryfhout, 9; Getty Images: John Cancalosi,
19, Roger de la Harpe, 3; iStockphoto: tirc83, 15; Science Source: Anthony Bannister, 21,
Yoshiharu Sekino, 7; Shutterstock: chamleunejai, 17, pashabo, Design Element, reptiles4all,
11, Ryan M. Bolton, 1, Skynavin, Cover, Steve Byland, 2, 5, Cover Back, Trahcus, 18;
SuperStock: Animals Animals, 12, NHPA, 16, Scubazoo, 14; Thinkstock: Mark Kostich, 13.

Printed in China by Nordica
0415/CA21500544
042015   008845NORDF15

TABLE OF CONTENTS

Springing into Action.......................................4

The Big Squeeze...6

Deadly Venom..8

Tasting and Tracking.....................................10

On the Attack...12

Catch Me If You Can!......................................14

Open Wide...16

Be Patient!...18

Climbing Trees..20

Amazing but True! 20

Glossary 22

Read More 23

Internet Sites 23

Critical Thinking Using
     the Common Core......24

Index 24

SPRINGING INTO ACTION

A rattlesnake rests in the sun on top of a dusty desert rock. The **predator** is quiet as a mouse scurries closer. Then the snake quickly **strikes** its **prey**. The mouse never saw the snake before the snake attacked.

Snakes eat many kinds of prey, such as mice, birds, and pigs. The diet a snake eats depends on its size. Big snakes can eat big prey. Smaller snakes eat smaller prey.

FACT
Brazil's Snake Island has so many deadly snakes that people are not allowed to live there.

predator—an animal that hunts other animals for food

strike—to attack quickly

prey—an animal hunted by another animal for food

THE BIG SQUEEZE

Constrictors use their size and strength to overpower prey. These snakes wrap their bodies around their prey. Then they squeeze the prey until it quits breathing.

The largest constrictor is the giant anaconda. This powerful predator can be more than 20 feet (6 meters) long and weighs 300 pounds (136 kilograms). It is strong enough to kill a jaguar.

yellow anaconda

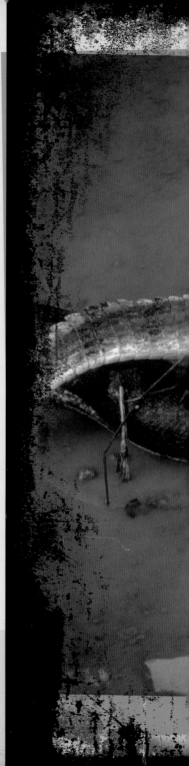

constrictor—a type of snake that wraps its body around prey and squeezes

An anaconda squeezes a caiman in Venezuela.

DEADLY VENOM

Not all powerful predators are large. Some **venomous** snakes are less than 2 feet (61 centimeters) long. But don't be fooled by their small size. These snakes kill their prey by **injecting** venom through their **fangs**. Rattlesnakes, vipers, and cobras are venomous snakes.

FACT

The inland taipan is the most venomous snake in the world. One bite from this snake produces enough venom to kill 250,000 mice!

venomous—able to produce a toxic substance called venom

inject—to put into

fang—a long, hollow tooth; venom flows through fangs

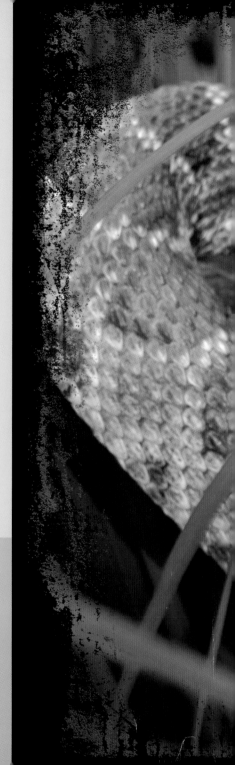

venom

TASTING AND TRACKING

Snakes use their sense of taste to find prey. A snake has a special body part in the roof of its mouth called a Jacobson's organ. It works with the animal's tongue to taste **particles** in the air. By flicking its tongue out, a snake can find and track its prey.

FACT

Pit vipers are venomous snakes that have holes in their faces. The holes help the snakes sense heat from nearby animals at night.

particle—a tiny piece of something

ON THE ATTACK

Snakes are known as **ambush** predators. They don't waste their energy chasing prey. Snakes stay still until prey is within striking distance. Then they strike in a quick motion. Most snakes can strike about half the length of their bodies.

death adder

FACT

The death adder **lures** its prey closer. The snake wiggles the worm-like tip of its tail to attract lizards and birds.

ambush—a surprise attack

lure—to attract something

CATCH ME IF YOU CAN!

Snakes can move fast. The black mamba can travel across land at 12.5 miles (20 kilometers) per hour. It can also strike quickly. Its amazing speed helps the snake catch prey. But like other snakes, black mambas wait for food to come close before attacking.

FACT
Sea snakes have flat tails that help them swim quickly to catch fish.

banded sea snake

black mamba

OPEN WIDE

Most snakes can eat animals several times wider than their own heads. A snake's jaws spread apart like rubber bands. This ability lets a snake swallow its prey whole. The green anaconda is the largest snake in the world. It eats wild pigs, deer, and even jaguars.

FACT

The easiest meal for a snake to eat is a smaller snake. This is because the animals are the same shape. But not all types of snakes eat other snakes.

green anaconda

anaconda

BE PATIENT!

Larger animals sometimes live for a short time after a venomous snakebite. Venom from some snakes **paralyzes** prey. The prey isn't able to breathe and dies quickly. Most snakes wait for the prey to die before eating it. Snakes can be hurt by eating prey that is still alive.

paralyze—to make someone or something unable to move

CLIMBING TREES

Snakes hunt in many ways. Some snakes even climb trees. They squeeze their muscles to hold onto the tree trunks. The black rat snake hides inside empty woodpecker holes. When a bird or other prey animal comes near, the snake quickly claims its victim.

AMAZING BUT TRUE!

Venom from the boomslang snake stops blood from **clotting**. A bite from this African snake can cause its prey to bleed to death. The prey dies quickly from the venomous bite, but the snake does not wait for it to happen. The boomslang begins eating right away.

clot—to become thicker and more solid; blood clots to stop the body from bleeding

GLOSSARY

ambush (AM-bush)—a surprise attack

clot (KLOT)—to become thicker and more solid; blood clots to stop the body from bleeding

constrictor (kuhn-STRIK-tur)—a type of snake that wraps its body around prey and squeezes

fang (FANG)—a long, hollow tooth; venom flows through fangs

inject (in-JEKT)—to put into

lure (LOOR)—to attract something

paralyze (PAY-ruh-lize)—to make someone or something unable to move

particle (PAR-tuh-kuhl)—a tiny piece of something

predator (PRED-uh-tur)—an animal that hunts other animals for food

prey (PRAY)—an animal hunted by another animal for food

strike (STRYK)—to attack quickly

venomous (VEH-nuh-mus)—able to produce a toxic substance called venom

READ MORE

Bishop, Nic. *Snakes.* New York: Scholastic Nonfiction, 2012.

Taylor, Barbara. *100 Things You Should Know about Snakes.* Broomall, Pa.: Mason Crest, 2011.

Woodward, John. *Everything You Need to Know About Snakes: And Other Scaly Reptiles.* New York: DK Pub., 2013.

INTERNET SITES

FactHound offers a safe, fun way to find Internet sites related to this book. All of the sites on FactHound have been researched by our staff.

Here's all you do:

Visit *www.facthound.com*

Type in this code: 9781491450390

Check out projects, games and lots more at
www.capstonekids.com

CRITICAL THINKING USING THE COMMON CORE

1. What do snakes eat? Does a snake's body limit the size of prey it can eat? (Key Ideas and Details)

2. What is a constrictor? How do constrictors hunt prey? (Key Ideas and Details)

INDEX

blood, 20

Jacobson's organ, 10

Snake Island, 4

snakes
  black mambas, 14
  black rat snake, 20
  boomslang, 20
  climbing, 20
  cobras, 8
  constrictors, 6
  death adders, 12
  diets, 4
  fangs, 8
  giant anacondas, 6

green anacondas, 16
inland taipans, 8
jaws, 16
rattlesnakes, 4, 8
sea snakes, 14
senses, 10
sizes, 4, 6, 8, 16
speed, 14
striking, 4, 12, 14
swimming, 14
tails, 14
tongues, 10
vipers, 8, 10

venom, 8, 18, 20